The May Anthology
of Oxford and Cambridge Poetry 1999

Varsity/Cherwell

First published in 1999 by Varsity Publications Ltd

ISBN: 0 902240 26 9

A CIP catalogue record for this book is available from the British Library.

Typeset by Suzanne Arnold
Produced by Origen Production Limited
Printed and bound in Great Britain

Original concept: Peter Davies, Adrian Woolfson, Ron Dimant

Further copies of this book are available from good bookshops in Cambridge and Oxford, or direct from Varsity Publications Ltd, 11-12 Trumpington Street, Cambridge, CB2 1QA

Editors: Benjamin Yeoh, Sophie Craig (Cambridge)
        Matt Edwards, Chris Tryhorn (Oxford)

Executive Editor: John Kinsella

Publisher: Suzanne Arnold

Cover Design: Alex Evans, Benjamin Yeoh

Cover Photos: Benjamin Yeoh

Editorial Committee: Sunila Galappatti, Tashi Lassalle, Ivana Mackinnon, Katie McAleese, Rana Molana, Debs Paterson, Elizabeth Prest, Heather Richards

Cambridge College Sponsors: Churchill, Clare, Corpus Christi, Darwin, Fitzwilliam, Gonville & Caius, King's, Jesus, Pembroke, Robinson, Queens', Sidney Sussex, Trinity

Oxford College Sponsors: New College, St Anne's, St Hugh's St John's, Templeton, Wadham, Wolfson

Thank you also to Carole Blake, Penguin Press, Hodder Headline, Dr Michael Franklin, Rachel Flowerday, Alex von Tunzelmann for their assistance

Contents

Introduction

Ambiguities

Questions of identity and locality come to the fore in an anthology based on a "transient" population. The years spent at university are, in the main, a geographic anomaly in the scheme of one's life. The notion of place is deeply informed by this temporal condition – where one is coming and going, the interaction between home – the location, country and culture one comes from – and "residence" – the culture that constitutes a specific College, or the hallmarks of the University as a whole. Home might be a village in the North, or the city of London, or mid-America, or Delhi. Wherever. Each poet has his or her own sense of place. But in the environment of exchange and interaction that the university provides, these notions of identity are in flux and come into question. One potentially looks at where one comes from in a different light. This creates a dynamic that is energetic and fascinating. Cross-pollination, cultural interface, the public life and the hermetically private, the historical and the spontaneous, all meld to form a poetics that this anthology locates as the face of Cambridge and Oxford poetry.

A sense of history is a strong binding force but, as many of these poems show, the drive is as external to Oxbridge as it is generative in its terms. What is particularly noticeable is the interdisciplinary nature of the poetry – one gets the feeling that these poems are written by students with a wide variety of interests. And the selection I have made from the shortlist prepared by the student committees is intended to reflect both diversity and a common sense of purpose, a deep concern with what makes language and the mechanics of a poem work.

There is a strong awareness here of what constitutes a poetic "voice", and a sound knowledge of both traditional and innovative verse techniques. These are poets who are able to make acute and vivid sensory observations, while being aware of literary tradition/s – often playing against them in complex and ironic ways.

One of the characteristics of this anthology as a whole is the sense of "ambivalence" that is evoked in the poems. Ambiguities are created by the poets to draw the reader (or listener) into the poetic process. At times disturbing, such as in the poem 'The Varieties of Religious Experience', the voices within the poems challenge the voice of the poets themselves. There are a number of vivid portraits painted here, such as in 'Annie Owen' and 'Aunt Fay's Undoing'. There is also an ethical drive to most of the poems, especially in the darkly ironic "anti-politics" of 'The Trigger'.

The range of technical devices used to qualify this dynamic between the voice of the poet and the voice of the poem is astonishing. From the pastiche in 'Midnight Mass' through to the sestina form of 'Colonies', the "intertextual" spreadsheet of 'Peccavi' and the verbal density of 'Fending Off'. There is a strong consciousness of what constitutes the "lyrical I" and the implication of the "confessional" voice. Witness 'leaving time' and the deconstructive word play of 'Drinking String'. The wonderful 'It is Difficult To Eat' deploys a metatextual conceit that undoes itself. It is a poem playfully examining the critical and creative processes.

Two poems that are both disturbing and carefully handled, are 'Assumption (detail)' and 'The Devil's Interval'. The latter, with its elegiac beauty and determined undoing of the "romantic" gesture towards "experience", burns with its contradictions and ambiguities. 'Assumption (detail)', captures the tension between the physical and the spiritual:

> someone must always be left,
> feet firmly in dust,
> to watch the ascent.

These are poets who have been left to watch the ascent of language each with a different way of "voicing" their experience. The geographies are different, but the points of focus are shared.

JOHN KINSELLA
March 1999

leaving time

something, you think,
in the way leaves lie at 7am.
sift through them

across the park: it must
be jazz, their not-quite-
settled-yet improv-

isation, vibrating as
they scatter at the bass-
line of your feet.

such harmony, the way
they've waited all night too,
arranging their jagged

edges to your tune. is it
– organic? – a rhythm? to think
it links us across miles

of london: that the pattern
of our leaves works out
the same. i'm a little

displaced, but for once
i think i know you,
and, too, the reassuring news

that we are not androids.
compare it to whatever
you kicked up last night.

then would you share it? listen.
the beats recede.
bethnal green. you're going

home. as you lean forward
on the tube and
wilt to sleep, know this:

i went ahead, alone, hands full
of leaves. i composed
a prelude to your dreams.

ADAM BARNARD

The Trigger

Imagine if your parents' days exploded out of seventies screens like a mushroom cloud
When fear of the cold became its own instant oblivion of friends in disintegration
Two fingers on triggers held the world's breath as it turned without reason
Because they recalled the Wars of forefathers when they won and lost
And never believed the bomb to be capitalism just against communism
It was the defence of three million fingers on triggers in bloody fields
Brothers falling away apart in foreign lands all for unknown civilians
I start with a shot in an Italian bar fashioned in the old King's Arms
And hypothesise while having a blast among slurring drunks' faces
We slip slowly about and our big-bang theories hover purposelessly
I wonder where I stand sitting with my hand gripping the glass butt
Finger on the world's pulse I'll soon forget it and lay it somewhere else
The drums kick in like guns and bombs; happily I point the glass at my mouth

MATTHEW BOURNE

17

Drinking string

Between any two points don't we agree there is always a journey?

Outside these seeping edges
(from lip-liner bleeding)
there is me here, seething.

A binge – what begins with
burnt potato and cherried jam –
(all juices of country lashing, and coconut)
this of course being Freedom, sieved.

My lips are bare,   (not here)
and bitten.
Lower lip bitten.   (Here! bring in the crush-fruits.)

You're interlacing left over meals,
not as holy-hot as once they were…   (that's right.)
Swarmy marshmallow soup divides right
            through
Dividing Right, from Left over.

The-strength-to-resist-then-to s-t-r-e-t-c-h -
            (Here you go! here I go, here's my coming Pout)
Sickeningly, it
    Tricks me.
        Retchingly
            Elongated,
                Tarnished and
                    Covers-me-and-my-lining in
                        Ham-fruits. Ah!
                        (ah me; my coming Pout, coming out.)

Sweetened crushed-leaf: teas
rip. Open my mouth; these finish,
dry the tongue
and scar the bite.

Come here, come here, come *here come*... (shhh! here I'm nervous.)

These are my parts:
Nervous throat, bitten knees, a float of pain.
My bony knees and languid neck still skin me.

I will now yes let me: I'll
submit, thirsting
for milk and milk-waters.

To treacle and trickle
                    (in some ways to tickle)
into the edges of lining again.

Let me sip.
Slipping please let me into the stopped gap –

now sit;   hhhhh
and breathe;   hhhhh
and linger within, I sip.

Th*inner with*in, see
now that I drink.
Here – it is trickling String.

EDITH BUKOVICS

As Skin

As skin
memorizes the
  circle of a ring
and words
  breathe
the instinct
  of flowers
the way
  hair falls
in a part
of you
   re member
as skin
 remembers–
     touch.

ALLYSSA CASE

from *Pub Crawl*

I. Frog Hall

Five doors, nine gateposts down from the snicket,
Gilligan's sawing metal, packing more spark
than his rebellious kecks have done
in a lifetime, nearly igniting the privet.
If I could ride one tiny orange ricochet,
duck gravity and moment (or rewrite
them to suit myself), I'd do it, and
be my own copernicus for a day.

Most houses around here are accretions
of the tenants' very own baroque, which is mine too.
Ciaran's floods to the calf every January,
his punt-pole a yard brush, his compensation
tuppence. We embrace with the habitual caution
of the thin, fearful our ribs should enmesh
inextricably. He has in his pocket a packet
of toffees. Hard. I ask again to ride pillion.

Two pound for petrol? I let coin
drop into his hand. He tips the wink –
he is all capability, all vista, all.
All laughter, all language, once more leprechaun.
Our ride is turbulence as far as Peasholme Green
and Frog Hall. Three heads turn at our entry. Ciaran puts
all nine stone right behind me. TRIVIAL PURSUIT.
black backslanting on orange scintilla. MONDAYS 7 PM.

Oh aye? The middle head speaks. The intonation mandarin.
Tracey sits awry on her forty-seven years, and what with her
knee

badly, shouldn't be at this lark at all, at all. *Guinness, is it?*
She moves with economy, like a frigate, quite benign.
I know you, or used to. Aren't you Lynn Fawell's bairn?
Worked up at gliding club, married that engineer.
Snotty cow. Never cared much for her own.
I say: *My mam still flies.* Tracey sniffs and three-point turns.

Your friend has scarpered, she replies. Ciaran is gone.
We want no prophets in this place at all. I take my pint,
and join dapper 'Dickie' Bowe, who is digesting obituary.
Today is not propitious. He recognizes only one:

Him, his pleasures were weekly:
a bus across town
a bag of mint Imperials
and a pornographic film
but he liked the toilets best,
lavish crimson tile
and boothed attendant:
etiquette, economy
and relief. He'd turn left
as he went in, then twisting
his head right, kept watch for the attendant
who'd come goloshing in, meaty, simple
not knowing the meaning of solicit
but with piss-coloured eyes
full of malice and tears.
Anyway, our man, one week
stops going. The films were
all shafting in kitchens now
and yawping in foreign.
He'd liked them soundless
with a bit of scene-setting.
Farm-boys, or recruits.

He'd miss the lavs.
Next day he wakes up
eyes right, and stuck that way
and after a week of wry saluting
(those army boys!) goes to the doctor,
whose urine-sample eyes
and keen soft mouth diagnose the guilt
that our man never felt.
Dr. Craw suggests massage
and mentions homosexual rapport.
He replies: "For Pete's sake, doc, have some fucking savvy!
Can't you see it's useless unless it's in the lavvy?"

The rhyme hung there, meat on a hook.
I'll get my coat. Someone whispered *epiphany*
and didn't sing it, didn't. Ears cannot be shut.
Outside, I perched on a bollard; it shook.
The ooze-up water in the Vale of York
had filmed the streets and turned glass.
Scuts of snow entered my shoes at the ankle, but then:
a show-off whistle – *Moving Cloud* – Ciaran, his mark.

KIT FRYATT

Tale

The needle slid so smoothly
into my finger I couldn't tell
till blood stained the tiny dress.
I dropped the cloth on the windowsill,
squeezed the flesh of my finger
and watched blood swell, then spin
to snow beneath, melting a dark hole.

My daughter will be pale as the flowers
of ice on my window – and red
with the blood of my belly.
As night thickens, the pane mirrors
my face. The fire sank to ashes
hours ago. I shiver, feel her flutter inside me,
this child I will never know.

TESS THOMPSON

Fending Off

Stike-tracked and bunched in tufts, stand hard, stocky stems,
surging from
land to iron
hulks hauled in to the river
Plants and pontoons, rotting wood weeps, holding under foamy
moss
Bony gusts on water
Banks judder and crumble, soft giving underfoot
Heavy-jointed lop bridges skew and slip in the mire,
Oak fibres soaking, rivets rusted strain
Cool reeds rustle, wave laps, ducks flap from clump to tump
Air creaks around her, lacing her lungs as ice
Hooded flowers dull stamens drown in silth and sedge and wiry
grass
The soil sags into the walling ooze, heaping into the flow
Saplings naked sway, root cords pluck at the padding turf
Buildings crumple quietly, far chimneys drawl out smoke
wreaths vie with birds wheeling forever in cold streams
Dogs dog her, hares hare.
Damp air about her neck, strange glimmers in the sky
Nothing blooms in the stiff breeze – everything seethes shifts slips
jumbles, jostles, snakes feeling through burrs and tubers whorl
underfoot to catch her step, fumbling as knots stud the ground.
Girders slide through the sludge
Pods crack, buds popping russet and ochre spill and swarm while
branches tremble
Her mumbled words stall and she can only breathe.
Banks still tilt and sink resigned
The ebb slaps the plant stacks
and larvae sleep cold in dark bubbles and glands
Ivy creeps, as usual

Louder than the cars, a dim drone like frenzied bees
numbing in winter, feeling the water.
She stumbles on a hollow bay, a slow lagoon
and a steel hull humped and greened in sleep,
Canting, cradling amber growths and velvet spores. She
                                              stops and reels.
More than the wash, the sky looms silent
Grey and sweep and pressing clouds
Below the stream front skirls and dripping capsules bead
                                              the leaves
Red-hued air, wily ground, snaring waves
Prime evil nature could be alien
cold and crisp, drooping sunlight bleeds
Her eyes can't let it seep
Fungi cluster, moist bark slips her ape fingers.
The soft tundra drifts unyielding, the liquid sheet deceptive
                                              and dead
She's afraid and alone by the wash.

JACOB HARDERS

Have without having

Chivalric triangle of desires
winding corners, fleeting stairs,
the real opportunity

is really a game:
the infinite delay of consummation,
the annihilation of all

to the last drop of blood
and crazed, lucid sweat
in the fevered twist of linens.

The truth remains unrevealed
through countless confessions
bodies thin as angels

crawling, again, begging
back to the miserable seduction –
if only they'd relinquish

the desire
for the grasp, the stifling hug,
and have without having

that obscene thought
of love
without the branded cow's hide,

or choke of a pomegranate's endless seeds.
The daring to do nothing,
to wake at dawn and listen

and through listening,
through nothing,
hearing everything.

MIRANDA HODGSON

Aunt Fay's Undoing

For all his efforts, she never turned her face
from his, a lock of the neck's cogs or a
sick devotion, ailing focus on tiny motions
of Self she dressed as tenderness.

We couldn't watch. She wouldn't turn her back.

Show me my uncle I'll show you a man
whose will carved furrows through her
thick-wedged faith and yet she stayed.

And though he charges
in with cutting palms aloft to reduce her
to vegetable pulp, she justifies

"I am seized by the way you crush doubt
out of me   you are a rock in a vast sea
you open a door to the rush of wind
that smoothes my angles   carves me into
beauty   licks me into a reverie of soft repose."

We watched her crash in slow-motion
locked with him in a macabre dance,
a kind of crack-smiled martyrdom
or agony of subservience.

Not one of us could watch, but waved
our hankies to see her off.

TRIONA KENNEDY

Peccavi

An Instruction	The History of the Form

1: The Article

Confession is a glib art,
taught young in the dark
house of muttering.
Day long, heart-beaten.
Written.

2: The Faith

Not mine. Under-
Mined by hours of
Learning to bite my tongue,
wanting someone
else's; smell
Of incense; temptation.

3: Concession

You are always
In the wrong. Never
Apologise. No regrets.
Declare all goods.

4: Appropriation

The narrow box of custom,
his chest, a pillow. Groove of
Polished walnut. Somewhere
harder
than it looks. Cold sweat.

5: Application

I confess: truth is easy,
telling tales
my job.

It hates me.

6: The Telegram

India, an apology:
Peccavi.
Lord Ellen's trick of
a classical education
lost on us.
And found.

7: Empire

I, too, have Sind,
my one hot night –
two sweats, two skins.
A bed, sub-
continental.

8: The Trade

No spice.

9: (In)dependence

What else? A lie, a double
Dealing.
Intentional. International.
He (India) I (small as
Pakistan and tear-shaped)

Our skins, the Sind. Content–
ious, touching.

10: The Border

Nothing to declare, no
theft, no breakages, no forbidden
foreign objects. My bed
a narrow custom, glib
and true.

SOPHIE LEVY

Colonies

From here the settlement can look pretty,
anyone can walk down by the long bay
and circuit the shore as small boats trim
their sails before setting out close
to the edge of the sun path, to lead
the flotilla calls for brawn and nerves, stuff

I haven't got at all. My father's stuff
lies in the land, sour slopes, pretty
average for the coast, acidic, lead
deposits, silver, iron. A doubtful bay
of plenty as named by the explorer close
to the end of map and century, neat and trim.

On his chart of possible failure, no trim
or tinsel like road laced with clay and stuff
that soaks deep my splayed old boots at close
of day when I trudge and slump pretty
done in by hoe, barrow, and quite at bay
taunted by a father who would have a lead

on my neck, before giving me a coin of lead
at best, at worst he'd fetch a stick and trim
a line of flesh off my arse, Botany Bay
was never that bad, I do the convict stuff
down to a T, which in the right light is pretty
much the shape of the gallows, the close.

But getting morbid never works, close
is the day when the old man will lead
us down to the cemetery plot, pretty
as sin in a box. I'd like to trim
the grave with black rocks, his stuff
not mine, I'm off. Walk through the bay

and orange groves. Find a kitchen, with bay
marjoram and sweet sorrel, in jars, all close
to hand, all clean and polish, all stuff
that's useful and fine, a black lead
hob, iron pots and pans. I'd sit and trim
veg, sit back, survey, smells good and pretty.

Yet this bay swings round me as lead
held far too close in, with a clear trim
of fuck all. Stuff it, something could be pretty

LEO MELLOR

Pollen

"The mystery of who killed 32 men found in a mass grave in Germany in 1994 has apparently been solved by examining the victims' sinuses." (1 – Oct – 98)

Dating barbarity to a single flower
this has been my aim.

The crushed bag of the skull
can be eased then opened,
my instruments carve
and find the matt traces,
scraped onto slides to prove
that a line of reasoning
was written on flesh:
not March 45, the Ost front
but rather KGB 1953
exact, precise, just as dead.

Pollen lodged means it was hot
late June / July
they must have marched
through the meadow first,
plantain bulrush couchgrass,
each swayed enough
at the volley of shots from beyond the trees.

LEO MELLOR

Annie Owen

Wrapped in grizzled tissue
In an aged cardboard box
At the back of the cupboard under the stairs
Is a faded photo, ebbing at the edges.

Just a girl perched on a lap, grave as a beak.
I see it now and then, just by chance,
When a hanger falls, or the dust-brush goes missing;
It is there,
Waiting to warm memories into clarity –

And I'm back in Massey Avenue, aged seven,
In a sulky patchwork dress and a bad haircut,
In the front room with the clicking gas-fire
That makes the other rooms shiver.
And she's holding my head down tight,
Bristles dragging with inartistic vigour
As I am made neat to match the house.

There's the smell of Sundays in the kitchen,
Half-eaten weekend trifle on the sideboard,
Heavy velvet curtains behind the white net –
(Just right for playing in)
A big pot of twenty pences over there,
To buy me a flat now.

I am being snapped at lovingly,
And I am ignoring it because I know I can;
She's strict to the point of total laxity,
Which I exploit with artless guile,
Eating the food she cooks and chewing up all the
affection,
Because it is all mine.

I remember the irascible energy,
The biting eyes and the flashing tongue;
Irritability with a Welsh accent
But I glimpse moments of tenderness,
Some tentative declaration of fondness
Weaknesses as nonchalantly received
As the twenty pence pieces in the pot.

I only miss them now, as the picture pulls into focus,
And I think of the hospital room that came later,
With a gleaming bed and sick-green walls,
Ugly flowers and wilted ladies,
An awkward family and a listless skeleton;
Apathy without a voice.

The end ruined it for me, and for you too –
You are two people, and I prefer the first.
I didn't say it then,
Just sang, tuneless on your knee:
Though you may be far away, I still think of you.

BETH MORREY

The Varieties of Religious Experience

Of all the broken people in New Jersey,
He was the brokenest. Three nights in a row
I watched him sitting hunched on the same bar-stool
Trying to cadge drinks without saying a word,
Which isn't easy. I've seen plenty of people
With easier jobs who probably did them worse.
Even broken you could tell he'd been a big man
And must've broke hard: his face was scarred and grey,
With phony teeth and an upper lip like a camel's,
And you could read how the cheekbones had been crushed,
The nose too. How he looked like he'd been pushed
Up and down New Jersey when they laid the highways,
And after it all, that face was what was left.
Or after it all, New Jersey was what was left.
Whichever it was, when closing time came round,
He set off, limping, alone down the state road
That leads from Milville back to Fortescue.
Where I was driving, though I'd had more than a few.
And I pulled my rented pickup over, beckoned
To offer him a lift. He didn't smile.
He didn't even wave me on. He just kept walking.

So next night in the bar I got the story.

"You bought me a drink, guess you wanna hear the story.
Well, here you go. I used to ride a chopper,
You know, a *motorcycle* – full slammed dresser
With a 98-inch stroker, S & S,
And Ron Simms bags that'd ground at the canyons,
A full crane cam and panels by Arlen-Ness,
And a coupla Kennedy 80-spoke big wheels.

41

Cherry-red chassis. She was called the Redhead.
That was a chopper to raise hell with, and on.
I fucking *loved* her.
                        Anyhow, this one time
I'm taking her out through bumblefuck, cow country,
Down a twisty road with a ravine on the right-hand side,
And every so often a wooden sign, *Appel Farms*
Fifty Miles, or *Appel Farms Sixty Miles*,
Leans up from out the ravine, like a mop in a bucket.
And I'm coming up on the one says *Forty Miles*,
And I must've hit a patch of gravel, or something,
But there it was: the Redhead pulls up free
And sails off toward the signboard and the ravine.
And that's when I saw God.
                        But the way it went,
I don't remember anything for a week.
Then I wake up. And there's a doctor there,
And he's got some other dude in a coat and tie,
And he's got the chief of Millville police there too:
Smug little cocksucker, that one, Richard Kane.
And I'm in a cast, can't even turn my head,
And my arms and legs are sticking in the air,
And I ache like my bones've been chewed on by a dog.
Chief says to me, *Tommy, know what you were doing*
When you hit that patch? I says, *Riding my bike.*
Is there a law against that one, Ossifer Dick?
And I realize that as I'm talking I got no teeth.
He says, *No, Tom, how fast you were going, I meant.*
And when I don't answer, he just says to me, *Ninety.*
Ninety on a road made for twenty. A road made for cows.
I say, *If you were there to clock me at ninety,*
Why the fuck didn't you stop me and do me a favor?
He says, *Nobody clocked you, no-one was there.*
We know how fast you were going from the imprint

Your teeth left in that wooden signboard you hit.
No shit. They showed me it later, hunk of wood
With a big dent from my head, and there below
This little scooped-out row, like a fossil of shell –
My teeth, but delicate, like they got pressed in wax.
Then the doctor explains how I had died on the table,
How I bruised my heart in the accident, blah blah;
How lucky I was the Redhead caught fire and blew up,
Cause that attracted a coupla guys out fishing
Way down Cohansey Creek. Wasn't for them,
Nobody'd've found me till one of the farmers came
To see if he'd lost a cow where the birds were circling.

So they leave me with the guy in the coat and tie,
Who's a *therapist*. Who wants to know how I'll *cope*.
And all of a sudden I remember what all happened.
I remember how I saw God. I talk about that.
He looks at me kind of funny, but smiles, and tells me
There's a *group* for people who've been through this same
thing.
Now I don't go in for groups. I'm not the type.
But this sounds like some real shit, know what I mean?
Of course I want to meet other people who seen Him.
So I go to the group. Worst fucking night of my life.
Cause you know what? They're crazy, all of them,
A whole *federation* of frigging fruits and nuts,
That get their jollies pretending they been through
Something as awful as the things I been through;
There's freaks that think God phones them up at night,
And blue-haired ladies think He's got their cat,
Talking about the clouds and the warm golden light,
And former drunks who say, *God told me to stop drinking!*
That's what one of them says. And I'm just thinking
Funny how, with the Holocaust, God says nothing,

But He sounds off when this dude has a beer.
Just poor deluded motherfuckers, every last one.
You know how I know? Not one of them remembered
What did He look like. *I* remembered, though.
Not like that blue-eyed pansy in the nightgown
They show you in the pictures. He was dark and ugly,
With a broken nose, and lots of crinkly black hair.
His arms were big, though, like a construction worker.
He looked like a biker, a Hell's Angel or something.
Yeah, I *know*...
                                    But he talked to me the whole time.
Though I don't remember a single thing he said.
His voice was like music. Not like it was pretty –
It wasn't – but 'cause I followed it along
And it made sense, somehow, without *meaning* anything.
I listened to him the way a dog'll listen.
I missed the words but I caught the tone of his voice
And the tone of his voice was *mean*. He reamed me out,
That righteous son-of-a-bitch, like I was his bitch.
And then he left. Didn't vanish into the light.
He just kind of wandered out of my line of sight.
And I couldn't turn my head, cause by that time
They'd got my neck and my shoulders in that cast.
Yeah, it ticked me off to hear those losers talking
About their clouds and golden light, like God
Would do himself up like a frigging Hallmark card.
I don't get mad about it now. I know they *believe*
They saw something. I know it was real to them,
Even if it wasn't really real. What's that to me?
No skin off my pecker. I don't make any claims.
And I don't do shit for attention. I'm just a guy
With a fucked-up face and a set of plastic teeth
Who walks where he's gotta go. What could I do?
Got rods and plates in my arm, a plate in my head.

I'm useless as tits on a boar-hog now, no good
For anything but drinking. Smoke a little grass,
Sometimes I pick up a whore if I got the money.
And I tip her extra if I got the money.
But I don't ride a chopper anymore. You know.
I tried getting on one once, at a trade-show,
But it gave me the all-over shakes, and when I looked
My knuckles'd gone bone-white the way I gripped her."

PETER MORRIS

Midnight Mass

The organ's close-packed copse of pipes
    Unstops its gorgeous storm.
The pubs call time. The tipsy churchbells
    Tumble: *Come, O Come*

To the cave of candles and cold snow
    Our childhood used to know.
When shepherds watched their flocks, and snow
    Had fallen. Snow on snow.

In the beginning was the Word,
    As bright as any blood,
And Mary bore sweet Jesus Christ
    In the beginning. In the wood.

God so loved the world
    That he gave his only Son
Then earth stood hard as iron,
    Water like a stone –

In the bleak midwinter
    Emmanuel is come.
The priest prepares the sacrament.
    We won't go until we've got some,

So bring us the ox, the ass, and camel;
    The three wise men; their gifts; the three
Ships; the holly; the ivy;
    A partridge in a pear tree;

And come, ye merry gentlemen,
  Following yonder star –
Trip it featly, singing sweetly,
  Leave the church by the vestry door,

Follow twelve lords a-leaping
  Through the little town, on a midnight clear,
And through all the trees that are in the wood,

  To the rising of the sun, and the running of the deer.

JEREMY NOEL-TOD

'Hunched over...'

Hunched over, shovelling down your food
You look beautiful to me.
    Your naturalness warms my
    hardened veins. That moment when I can see you, drink
in every detail while you continue on,
                unaware.

The magic dies, though, when I sit down
because you notice me.
    Your striking honesty becomes
    guarded. Watched you change shapes, become a new
person. Still, you regard your food,
              not me.

Then, you break the peace, as well,
choosing to question me.
    Banishing silence. That friend
    has always been welcomed in my heart. Mutual regarding,
understanding can flourish in silence,
            not with speech.

That which is thought can be
perfect, unlike garbled
    speech. Forced questions
    and necessary replies defeat the purposes of honesty.
Convention, that damned bond, separates
           soul from soul.

Wretched in my solipsistic
throes, I am a horrible
    companion to you now
  when you want one. Please go back to that unguarded
state, shovel down your food. Be beautiful
            for me.

JAMES SCHUBRING

The Devil's Interval

When they dragged him from the water
they say the sea burst from his lips in a song –

that, where the waves had bitten his body
and the sun scorched his skin,
the sores opened to speak of his suffering

to recount the days before he was found.

But they could neither read the language
in these signs nor pronounce his death

an accident or suicide.

He was not alabaster white, like Shelley,
nor reposed in thoughtful stone
but swollen and burnt by the confluence
of night into day

his head, a corona of flies, and his clothes
trailing behind him like wings

skin the pallor of wax.

They say the sight of him sent a shiver
of sweat across their brows

despite the sultry afternoon sun

but they soon remembered themselves
and plucked death from the water

ripping tongues of meat from his chest
with their grappling irons
distending the symmetry of their nets.

On board, he lost some of his mystery

his wounds dried mud-red
youth stiffened into old age

and he looked out, eyeless, from a moon's face
mortality proving him no god.

His voice, however, remained like an enigma
curled up inside him like a stone.

* * *

It must have seemed quite different
when he walked, fully-clothed, into the sea
waiting for the water to disrobe him.

It had been a night so hot
even the waves fanned themselves
and the wind grew tired
sloughed off its skin, then lay in the dust.

The moonlight, when it emerged, seemed

like a woman's hand, slowly uncoiling
the rope of darkness from its anchor,
flesh

cooling first his muscle, then his bone,
soothing each sense in turn
before calming his heart's pulse, gradually.

Only, the undertow betrayed him

like an eel slipped between his legs
and looped him deeper, down, into darkness
coaxing him one step further
moving the ground beneath his feet

the constant beguilement of water.

Did he panic, then, to feel the current touch
him, snag his ankle, pull him
under

snare him in its long low trawling nets

or did he relax
to find his body suddenly weightless?

He had wanted to experience the devil's interval

to feel the sea lift him in each swell and drop him
moved, unmoved; to hear the breakers
surge overhead and leave him speechless
only his blood singing.

But he wanted more than this

to swim and dive in treble clefs, block his ears
to the air's applause, surrender
each breath to the rhythm
of the waves

and drink in the surrounding silence.

Perhaps it was the ghost in his lungs
that in the end betrayed him
the footsteps he didn't want to follow
that finally pursued him

the hourglass in his throat that capsized
then slowly filled with sand.

His friends, waiting for him on the shore,
had no idea

he could hold a note for so long…

MATTHEW SKELTON

Coming Home

Titanium white smudge of suggested face,
Inclined, slightly,
Kohl black eyes, eyelashes,
Swathe of scarlet hair
over just-there arc of darker shoulder.
More perfect
In the reflection
Of the window
Of the train,
New Street to Oxford (Diverted),
Than when I stare, rudely,
At the figure diagonally opposite,
Hair matted, roots showing dark,
Gold hoop over right eye,
Patches of shiny oily skin,
A paperback pointing my way,
Women On Women.
I want to speak to her,
Tell her how real she seems,
Hear her voice,
Woman to Woman.
Instead my eyes drift, politely, onto pylons,
Watching her enigmatic smile
Hurtle through the Midlands.

GEORGINA TAYLOR

It is Difficult To Eat

It is difficult to eat
A Satsuma
Whilst reading a book.
Sandwiches, providing they are not too full
Or made with stuff that falls out easily
(e.g. salad) are okay
Apples, biscuits, slices of cake too.
The Satsuma
Demands
Both hands
For peeling.
The peel creates an added problem because you have to put
it somewhere, and
Peeling The Satsuma has already put you off reading your
book. A trip to the bin
Further defers.
(The problem is worse
with a hardback which occupies your knee where the peel
needs to go).

You can pick up your book again
But put it down immediately to break off
Segments. It is possible to perfect this with one hand
(I had Six Satsumas for the purpose)
But unless you are extremely dextrous
You can't peel off the white stringy bits
And even if you can you'll only keep losing your place in
your book.

In this way
Satsumas (clementines and other lesser derivatives)
Force us to devote
Our entire attention to them

Prevent us from reading –
And, when you think about it, all other two-handed activities –
While we have to absorb ourselves in them
Even before we can start to eat them.
Sainsbury's sells Satsumas in
Sixes, twelves, twenties, with
25% Extra Free.
How much time peeling 25% Extra Free's worth could
                                        otherwise be spent reading?
You can always peel, de-string and break into segments
Before you pick up your book
But that looks to me like obsession.
Unlike breaking up Six Satsumas with one hand which is
                                                            plainly
Research.

AMBER THODY

Assumption (detail)

I.

The apostles in Titian's *Assumption*
do not look to heaven.

Jesus rises above them, eyes turned upward,
hands outstretched. Already,
his blue and red robes hold light
like stained glass.

On the ground, apostles gaze up,
not to heaven, but to Him. One shades
his eyes. Another reaches
after Him, but his hand cannot catch
the hem of that robe.

II.

One will be taken and the other left.

When God found my mother, she was forty-three,
drinking during gaps
of the day when no one saw. God drew her up
out of shadows into sharp-edged
light. Sometimes I wish that she'd still fight
with me – but she prays, reads scripture,
needs nothing from me.

I have come to set a man against his father,
a daughter against her mother.

I know how the apostle felt, his instinctive
grasp at that cloth as he tried
to drag Jesus back to earth. But no:
someone must always be left,
feet firmly in the dust,
to watch the ascent.

TESS THOMPSON

Notes on Contributors

Adam Barnard's literary career began at the age of six when his experimental short story *The Boy Who Pulled An Aeroplane Down From The Sky With A Really Big Magnet* was acclaimed as "good work" by his teacher, Miss Anna. A long-awaited follow-up, *What I Had For Breakfast This Morning*, was less well-received, condemned as badly written: "This is messy. You aren't writing all your letters the same size." Adam never quite recovered from this blow and an extended (12-year) period of writer's block followed, which may or may not now have ended. An apparent computer error led to the award of a place at Queens' College, Cambridge, where Adam is reading books.

Matthew Bourne: Ex-teenager. Writer. Film-maker. Experimenter. Bullshitter.
Laborious student, Oxon. Belongs to London. Clinging on. Unpublished. Disbelieved. Biography-less. Reprieved.

Edith Bukovics is a second year undergraduate studying English literature at St Catharine's College, Cambridge. Originally Viennese, she has since hustled between numerous countries and thrives on the inspiration of different cultures. Trying to continue the many interests that distract from her BA degree is a full-time job, and one which conveniently confuses any career 'plans'.

Allyssa Case A recent Canadian import, Allyssa is an MPhil student in International Relations and a member of Darwin College, Cambridge. Before her trip across the pond, she completed a BA in English Literature at the

University of Ottawa.

Kit Fryatt was born in Tehran in 1978. She lived in Singapore and Turkey before returning to Britain to attend a convent school in Letchworth. She is now in the third year of an English degree at Peterhouse and plans later this year to move to Dublin to study and write.

Jacob Harders' main interests are acting and writing, therefore his perfect career would be acting in plays he has written. As things are, he enjoys playing bit parts and having his works rejected by publishers. He occasionally studies Classics.

Miranda Hodgson Up until now, Miranda Hodgson's biggest claim to literary fame was as a Researcher-Writer for the best-selling budget travel guide *Let's Go: Britain and Ireland 1996*. She graduated *magna cum laude* from Harvard University with a BA in English in 1997, and is currently a first year graduate student at Oxford, studying Old English and Norse with feminist theory.

Triona Kennedy's ambition is to live dreams and save the world. She eats cake and makes up devised dance theatre. She is in no rush to be a fabulous young writer, hoping sustained talent will settle with experience. Triona is wholly pleased that people will read this poem and the one in the 1996 edition. She has 'issues' about writing in the third person, no time for irony without balls, and takes joy in her English degree at Churchill College, Cambridge.

Sophie Levy, Corpus Christi, English second year. She has somewhere between far too much and never enough time on her hands and spends whatever there is of it writing. Her work has appeared in *Spark*, *InPrint*, *Quaypool* and she is the winner of the 1999 *Kinsella/Ryan* prize.

Leo Mellor is a tall and thin Brightonian.
Winner of the Rylands Prize, his first collection is published by Folio this summer.
Read in the dark / breathe water.

Beth Morrey is a finalist at Newnham College, studying English. She has acted in, and produced, several plays in Cambridge and is Co-Vice-President of the Cambridge Footlights.

Peter Morris graduated from Yale University and is now studying at Somerville College, Oxford. Peter is an editor of *Zero*, a literary magazine at Oxford. In 1998 Peter's play *The Square Root of Minus One* won first prize in the International Student Playscript competition, awarded by Sir Alan Ayckbourn.

Jeremy Noel-Tod is an English finalist at New College, Oxford. He lives in Dereham, Norfolk.

James Schubring, currently a visiting student at St Peter's College, Oxford, will graduate next year with a BA in English and American Literature from Harvard University. He hails from the dry, barren reaches of Montana and finds the English grin-and-bear-it attitude to daily rain a novel approach to life. This is his first publication.

Matthew Skelton is a graduate student at Somerville College, Oxford. He plans to finish his DPhil by September 2000 and hopes immediately thereafter to fall in love. He likes photography, cats, and the novelist Henry Green, but dislikes just about everything else. He was born in England, brought up in Canada, but doesn't know where he'll end up next. The expression 'Devil's Interval' may refer to the distance between two notes – one high, one low – in a piece of music. But, tone-deaf, the author doesn't quite know whether this is true (he once heard it in a lecture and thought it would make a brilliant title). The poem was written partly in response to Jeff Buckley's death.

Georgina Taylor I'm a student at Wadham College, Oxford, currently studying for a PGCE in secondary English teaching. Before that I studied for a DPhil in English, also at Wadham, focusing on a group of twentieth century women writers including H D (Hilda Doolittle), Muriel Rukeyser, Bryher and many others. My MA was in Creative Writing at Lancaster University, where I wrote a novel (*Passageways*) and a collection of poetry.

I found that my DPhil left me with little time or energy for my own writing, but now I'm enjoying recovering from that and getting back into my own writing. I feel that I'm at a bit of a transition point in my writing and am experimenting with new voices and ideas – the poems I submitted for the *May Anthologies* are a mixed bunch! My work has previously appeared in the little magazines *The Cracked Mirror* and *Em*.

Amber Thody is a final year English student at Churchill College, Cambridge. Her main influences include her grandma, being friends with non-arts students, and the Muppets. Like all proper English students, she will be training as a teacher next year.

Tess Thompson I have had poetry published in *Tempus*, *Byline*, and *Calyx, A Journal of Women's Art and*

Literature, and fiction published in *Seventeen*. I'm in the second year of the MPhil in English Studies; my undergraduate degree is from The Pennsylvania State University. I'm currently at work on a novel.